THE BERLIN WALL

A BRIEF HISTORY FROM BEGINNING TO END

HISTORY ENCOUNTERS

History of

The Berlin Wall

A Brief History from Beginning to the End

History Encounters

CONTENTS

Get it Now

Chapter One
Introduction

After the end of the Second World War, Berlin was split between the East and the West. The Western countries occupied the Western part of Berlin, and the Soviet Union occupied the East portion. It divided Berlin into two sectors from when it was built in 1961 to when it was broken down in 1989.

While this division was originally on paper, increasing antagonism between the Soviet Union and the Western allies during the initial fifteen years of the Cold War. Thereafter the Soviets took the decision to build an actual barrier between the two sides of Berlin. In this way, they created a solid Iron Curtain to replace the symbolic one that had been the division between East and West since after the end of WWII in 1945.

The primary function of the Berlin Wall was to deter East Germans from leaving to go to the West, thus halting a potentially economically dire migration of laborers, which would have crippled the already troubled economy. The Berlin Wall was officially called the "Anti-Fascist Protective Wall" by the authorities in East Germany. This implied that the NATO countries and the West Germans were fascists, unlike the communist Soviet Union.

Once the East-West sector border was closed in Berlin, the greater majority of East German citizens could no longer emigrate to or even travel to West Germany. Berlin went from being a reasonably straightforward spot to making an illegal crossing from East and West, too, arguably the riskiest and most challenging. Many households and families were divided and unable to visit one another, while East Berliners employed in West Germany could not return to their jobs.

The Berlin Wall was a formidable barrier. Construction started on August 13, 1961, and the Wall entirely isolated West Berlin from the surrounding area, which was in East Germany, and from East Berlin. Government officials opened it in November 1989. Its demolition took almost two years, beginning in June 1990. The original barrier consisted of guard towers which were positioned along massive cement walls, encircling a broad area. This became known as a "death strip," and it contained "fakir beds," which were beds of sharp nails on the walls, anti-vehicle trenches, and additional defenses to deter attempted escape. The Soviet Union alleged that the Wall was built to safeguard the population from Western fascist components, contriving to discourage people from producing a socialist state in East Germany. In reality, though, the Wall curbed the enormous problem of defection and emigration that had occurred in the years before the wall was built.

The Wall, which later became known as the Wall of Shame, stood as a physical symbol of the ideological Iron Curtain. Before the wall was built, almost 3.5 million people defected to West Germany. During the time of the Wall, almost all emigration was halted. More than 5000 people tried to escape, and the death toll stood at close to 200.

The Berlin Wall, to this day, causes anger and resentment among those descendants whose families were affected by the barrier and the ideology that underpinned it.

Chapter Two

The Timeline of the Wall

The Partitioning of Berlin

As World War II ended in 1945, the Allied peace conferences at Potsdam and Yalta specified the destiny of Germany. They divided the vanquished country into four "allied occupation zones": The eastern part of Germany went to the USSR while the western area went to the USA, Britain, and (after a delay) France.

Although 1961 was the year the Wall was first constructed, the circumstances that preceded its building began just after the conclusion of WWII in 1945. The Berlin Airlift, which happened between 1948 and 1949, where the Soviet Union would not allow supplies into West Berlin, and the allied powers were forced to bring them in on plane charters, was the landmark circumstance that signaled the heightened divide between the Soviet Union and the Western Allies.

Both German states, which were developed postwar, were established the year the Berlin Airlift ended in 1949. The former Russian occupation area proclaimed on 7 October 1949 was called the German Democratic Republic (GDR). Some months earlier, the other Allied sectors had become the FRG or the Federal Republic of Germany. Hitler's goal to expand Germany had now proved a colossal failure as Germany became a divided country, preparing for the arrival of "die Berliner Mauer," which would be an ugly blot on the German landscape for twenty-seven years.

The Berlin Wall Timeline from 1945-1989

- 1945 In late April, the Soviet troops entered Berlin. This indicated that World War II was just about over.

- 1945 German troops conceded defeat on 2 May.1945 The Potsdam Conference took place south of Berlin from 17 June to 2 August. The Allied conquerors - Great Britain, the USA, the Soviet Union, and France- divided Berlin and Germany into four occupation areas.

- 1948 On 24 June, the Berliner Blockade started. The Soviets cut off all transit routes operating between West Germany and Berlin. This turned West Berlin into a solitary island in hostile East Germany. With all land entry now obstructed, the Allies began the Luftbrücke or Berlin Airlift on 26 June. For the following months, Berlin was stocked by aircraft. All essentials, from food to coal, had to be airlifted into the city.

- 1948   By September, the Soviet Union forced the Berlin city "Stadtverordentenverwaltung B" to leave the "Red City Hall" in the east district. The communists divided Berlin based on the declaration of their "magistrate."

- 1949 On 12 May, the Soviets lifted the siege, but the Airlift continued until late September.

- 1949 On 23 May, the Federal Republic of Germany (Bundesrepublik) was founded in West Germany. This was closely followed by the German Democratic Republic (Deutsche Demokratische Republik in East Germany on 7 October. The capital city of West Germany was Bonn, but East Germany announced East Berlin as its capital.

- 1953   The well-known Workers Revolt of 17 June occurred throughout East Germany. Workers went on strike to insist on better labor and living circumstances. They also wanted free and fair elections and a union with West Germany. Soviet Union armies assisted the GDR in crushing the rebellion cruelly.

- 1955 The Allied countries declared Germany a sovereign nation on 5 May, ending their occupation.

- 1961 In an endeavor to halt the rising numbers of people fleeing the GDR, Walter Ulbricht, the Supreme leader, commanded the building of the Berlin Wall. On 13 August, East German forces and laborers began setting up barbed wire barriers that would ultimately become the Berlin Wall. The wall encircling Berlin would extend 100 miles (165 km). Berlin was a city torn apart, and East Berlin was a prison for its citizens.

- 1963 On 26 June, John F. Kennedy, the US president, made his famous "Ich bin ein Berliner," promising his solidarity with Berlin. Martin Luther King visited the following year, also declaring solidarity and support.

- 1971 An agreement signed on 17 December made it simpler to travel to Berlin.1973 Walter Ulbricht, the leader of the German Democratic Republic, died on 1 August.

- 1982 US president Reagan visited Berlin for the first time on 11 June.

- 1986 On 5 April, a bomb killed two US soldiers and another person in a disco called La Belle. Two hundred thirty people, of whom 50 were American, were also wounded in the terrorist explosion. The attack was blamed on Libya, which paid compensation, but the East Berlin police were also implicated.

- 1987 During a second visit to Berlin, US president Reagan made an impassioned speech at the Brandenburg Gate demanding, "Mr. Gorbachev, tear down this Wall!"

- 1989 On 19 August, more than 700 GDR refugees crossed the Hungarian-Austrian border.

- 1989 In October, the East German administration came under significant pressure to impose reforms. On 4 October, there were huge anti-government rallies, and the party leader Erich Honecker was forced to resign. On 23 October, the "Monday Demonstrations" began in the city of Leipzig. Chanting the motto "Wir sind das Volk!" which means "We are the people!" East Germans demanded revolutionary reforms and the government to resign.

- 1989 On 7 and 8 November, the GDR government resigned.
- 1989 On 9 November, the border was erroneously opened; effective immediately, a flood of people stormed the border and forced their way through. People began to knock the wall down systematically.
- 1990 In February, artists from 21 countries gathered to establish the East Side Gallery, which runs along a section of the Wall. It was all over at last.

Chapter Three

The Building of the Wall

It was a sullen crowd of German builders and workers who began the building of the Berlin Wall on 15 August 1961.

Why a Wall?

Just a few days after cutting off unrestricted passage between East and West Berlin with a fence of barbed wire, the East German administration began constructing a wall. The Berlin Wall was intended to close off access to West Berlin forever. For the following twenty-eight years, the strongly fortified Wall was a brick-and-mortar symbol of the burgeoning Cold War. It was an actual "iron curtain" dividing the city.

After the end of World War II, Germany was divided into Allied occupation areas. There were four of these. The German capital, Berlin, was also divided into occupation zones, even though the city was situated deeply in Soviet territory. The future destiny of Berlin and Germany was a primary point of contention in the postwar talks, and friction was evident when, in 1948, the USA, Britain, and France combined their territories into one independent entity. This was called the Federal Republic of Germany. In reaction to this, the Soviet Union undertook to blockade West Berlin to compel the West to withdraw from the city and leave it in Soviet hands. Nonetheless, an enormous airlift scheme by the United States and Britain kept the West Berliners stocked with food and petrol. In May 1949, the Soviet administration gave up on the unsuccessful blockade.

By 1961, tensions between Russia and the West concerning Berlin were escalating. The dissatisfied East Germans hating life under a communist regime saw West Berlin as a gate to the West and democracy. Between the period 1949 to 1961, millions of East Germans escaped from the East into West Germany, mainly via the West Berlin gateway. By August 1961, as many as 2,000 East Germans crossed into the West daily. Many of these defectors were skilled professionals, partisans, and academics, and the effect on the East German economy was devastating. To control the exits, Soviet president Nikita Khrushchev advised the closure of all access between East and West Berlin.

The Brick and Mortar Curtain

On the nights of 12 to 14 August 1961, East German troops established a 30-mile barbed wire obstacle through the middle of Berlin. East Berlin residents were prohibited from passing into West Berlin, and the number of border posts from which Westerners could cross into East Berlin was hugely reduced.

The West, surprised by this aggressive move, threatened to impose trade sanctions against the East to retaliate. The Soviet Union responded by setting up another land blockade of West Berlin and, emboldened by the lack of real reaction from the West, closed off more and more checkpoints. On 15 August, they started putting concrete in place of the barbed wire. The East German government claimed that the wall would preserve their citizens from the destructive impact of capitalist decadence.

According to histroy.com, "The first concrete pilings went up on the Bernauer Strasse and at the Potsdamer Platz. Sullen East German workers, a few in tears, constructed the first segments of the Berlin Wall as East German troops stood guarding them with machine guns." As the borders closed and security was heightened within its vicinity, East Germans defectors felt that time was of the essence and escaped by August 15. A now-iconic image of the Berlin Wall features the 19-year-old Conrad Schumann, an East German Soldier who was immortalized in a photograph of him "leaping over the barbed-wire barrier to freedom."

In 1961, the awful and hideous Berlin Wall proceeded to grow until it consisted of a string of 15-foot-high cement walls. These walls were capped with barbed wire and patrolled by men in the watchtower with machine guns. They were also surrounded by mines. By 1980 this network of electrified fences and walls was 28 miles in length through

Berlin and extended for 75 miles around West Berlin, effectively cutting it off from the remainder of East Germany. The East Germans also built a vast barrier along much of the border between themselves and West Germany.

The Berlin Wall was seen among the Western powers as a critical symbol of oppression from a communist regime. Approximately 5,000 East Germans escaped across the Wall to West Berlin, but successful escapes became more uncommon as the fortifications of the wall grew. Thousands of other East Germans were apprehended during these attempted escapes, and 191 were killed while trying.

In 1989, the borders were finally opened, and jubilant Berliners were free to mingle again.

Chapter Four

Ten Interesting Facts about the Wall

At least 5,000 people were able to flee East Germany either over or under the Berlin Wall, that iconic symbol of Soviet collapse.

- **Fact 1:** The Berlin Wall fell by mistake.

  At a news conference on the night of 9 November 1989, an East German official called Günter Schabowski made a premature announcement that constraints on getting visas to travel to West Berlin would be lifted. When he was asked when the new policy would be enforced, he erroneously declared, "Immediately, without delay." The policy was only meant to be announced the next day and would still have stringent visa requirements. This mistaken message meant that thousands of East Berliners stormed to the Wall. The few guards, including Jäger, the chief officer on duty receiving no credible instruction, opened the border gate and people streamed through into unplanned freedom.

- **Fact 2:** The Berlin Wall was only built more than 15 years after the start of the Cold War.

  At least two million East Germans, mostly skilled workers, academics, and professionals, escaped to the West between '49 and '61. The Soviet Union initially opposed East Germany's petition to erect a wall in 1953. Still, once people defecting into West Berlin reached more than 1,000 people daily by 1961, the Soviet leader Khrushchev capitulated. The citizens of Berlin were roused on 14 August 1961 to find that barbed wire fencing was established on the city border. This was followed by concrete notifications.

- **Fact 3:** The Berlin Wall was actually made of two walls.

  The 27-mile piece of the boundary wall, which separated Berlin into the east and west sections, consisted of two cement walls. Between these walls was a "death strip" up to which was as much as 160 yards wide in places, and it contained significant numbers of watchtowers, guard dog runs, anti-vehicle trenches, trip-wire machine guns, and " bright as day" floodlights.

- **Fact 4:** At least 138 people perished trying to escape across the Berlin Wall.

  These people were killed by bullet fire, fatally injured, or committed suicide after failing to escape. The final fatality happened in 1989 when an East German man was trying to fly a hot air balloon over the wall and crashed into electric power lines.

- **Fact 5:** More than 5,000 people managed to escape by going over and under the Berlin Wall.

An example of their commitment to escape is seen in Wolfgang Engels, who was an East German soldier. He had initially helped build barbed-wire fences that preceded the wall building and separated both sections of Berlin. He stole a tank and crashed through the wall in it, getting caught in the carved wire and shot, but he still managed to escape.

- **Fact 6:** John F. Kennedy was relieved when the Berlin Wall was built.

In 1961, President Khrushchev warned John F. Kennedy that he would barricade West Berlin if the Western armies did not withdraw. This aggressive act could have led to war. That is why Kennedy was relieved when he heard that the Soviets had walled in East Berlin instead of blockading it. West Berlin, he commented, "It's not a very nice solution, but a wall is a hell of a lot better than a war. This is the end of the Berlin crisis. The other side panicked—not we. We're going to do nothing now because there is no alternative except war."

- **Fact 7:** President Kennedy, despite the urban legend, did not, in fact, tell Berliners he was a "jelly donut."

On 26 June 1963, Kennedy apparently addressed a crowd at the Wall with the words "Ich bin ein Berliner." In Berlin, a donut was called a Berliner, but it's very unlikely that anyone seriously thought that's what the President meant.

- **Fact 8:** East Germany justified the wall by referring to it as an "Antifascist Bulwark."

  Rather than admitting the wall was to keep its citizens in, the East German authorities contended they had built the Berlin Wall to protect their people from Western fascist ideas and spies. Two weeks after authorizing the building of this "Antifaschistischer Schutzwall," the East German leader Walter Ulbricht contended that "We have sealed the cracks in the fabric of our house and closed the holes through which the worst enemies of the German people could creep."

- **Fact 9:** The Brandenburg Gate, which was a central feature of the Wall, had been a part of the wall since the 1700s.

  The Prussian King Frederick William II authorized the building of the significant and inspirational triumphal arch which straddled East and West Berlin. This was the significant backdrop for famous speeches by both Presidents Kennedy and Ronald Reagan. When this was completed in 1791, the Brandenburg Gate was integrated into it and later into the Berlin Wall.

- **Fact 10:** A fragment of the wall is part of the bathroom decor in a Las Vegas casino.

  The authorized demolition of the Berlin Wall started in 1990. More than 40,000 sections of the wall were converted into building equipment and material for German reconstruction programs, but some hundred portions were auctioned and are now dispersed across the world. One is in the Vatican gardens, but the strangest is in the men's bathroom of the Main Street Station Casino, where the urinals are erected on a graffiti-covered segment of the wall, fortunately, protected by safety glass.

Chapter Five

How the Wall caused Confusion among West Berliners

It's easy to think, bearing in mind the relatively few fatalities throughout the Berlin wall's life, that it did not cause the devastation that other periods of history did, but it certainly added to the toll of human misery already inflicted by years of war and ignominious defeat.

Barb's Story

Barb Dignan remembers the night the construction of the Wall began. She was fourteen, the daughter of an Army Major. She was not personally affected by the situation, but many of her friends and neighbors had people on the other side of the wall, and rumors were rife about being unable to contact East Berliners and even horrific gossip that all East Berliners were going to be killed. There was a terrible feeling of loss. People realized that without any warning, many of their friends and relatives were lost to them for good.

Tina Bain's Story

British Tina Bain visited a pen-friend in Berlin when she was fifteen. She was there when the construction began, and an atmosphere of panic, food stockpiling, and anxiety about their family being unable to contact them. There were tanks in the streets and a general feeling of panic.

Tina's pen pal Elke asked her to come back to Berlin in 1990 to celebrate the ending of the wall, which was a great occasion, and she enjoyed physically breaking down. Piece of the Wall herself.

Petra Tobihn's and Sebastian Merrick's stories.

As a child, Petra was distressed to hear that her father's children from his first marriage were on the other side of the wall and had not been seen by him for many years.

Sebastian Merrick was haunted by the stories of his Aunts who lived near the wall. He was particularly disturbed by 'der Todestreifen' or death strip. It seemed impossible to escape across that strip policed by guards and fierce dogs. He heard of people swimming along the river border, but even that was fraught with hazards.

British soldiers placed a swimming pool-type ladder on the river bank marking the border to assist people who swam across the river to escape—the East. The river was policed by armed soldiers in boats which made escape very difficult.

Manny Reyes compares West and East Berlin.

Manny Reyes, as a foreigner, could travel between East and West Berlin. He explained that West Berlin was like any other capitalist city in the world, but East Berlin was run down with buildings still peppered with bullet holes from WWII. The officials were hostile and threatening, and "Verboten" signs forbidding people to take photographs of the graffiti on the wall meant what they said.

The wall was a constant reminder to all these visitors to West Berlin that there was something sinister happening across the border that they could not fully understand and that was being kept secret by an oppressive regime.

Bonus Download

Want to Fill Your Digital Library for Free?

Every purchase comes with FREE bonus downloads! Download yours now by clicking the 'Get it Now' button.

Get it Now

Chapter Six

Daring Escapes

Despair drove invention among East Germans desperate to reach West Berlin. The ways they tried and often succeeded in escaping were very creative.

The first escapee to cross the Wall was a young East German sentry Conrad Schumann, who was filmed leaping over a high stretch of barbed wire just a couple of days after East the border from East Germany was sealed.

As the Berlin Wall became a fortress, escape plans became more elaborate. Deserters escaped in hidden car compartments, rescued by West Berliners. They dug tunnels and crept through the sewerage.

The Bethke brothers

The three brothers escaped in spectacular ways. The eldest Ingo floated on a blow-up mattress crossing the Elbe River. His brother Holger, eight years later, used a steel cable fired onto a rooftop with a bow and arrow to sail over the wall.

Finally, in 1989 the brothers flew a light plane back over the Berlin wall and picked up Egbert, their youngest brother.

Intrepid train engineer Harry Deterling kidnapped a steam train and rode through the final East Berlin station, saving 25 passengers by freeing them to the west.

Tunnels were also a courageous method of escape, and people from both sides tried to dig them. Lots were left incomplete or failed, but there were some successes. One particular student-built tunnel allowed 57 people to escape before the authorities got wise to it.

When people escaped in daring ways, they found a loophole that the East German government had to seal quickly.

Ida Siekmann and other Tragedies.

Ida Siekmann was the first tragedy of the wall. She was blocked into her apartment when police bricked up the door. The front of her building was in West Berlin. She did not wish to live in East Berlin, so she threw all her possessions and bedding through the Window into West Berlin and jumped. Unfortunately, she was so severely injured that she died en route to the hospital.

Many others were equally unlucky. One hundred forty people perished at the Wall or were executed for trying to cross the border. Another 251 travelers also died crossing checkpoints or border posts. No one knows how many people died from personal distress, loneliness, and despair after their lives were disrupted in this shocking way.

Between '61 and '89, many thousands of East Germans made hazardous attempts at crossing the border. At least 5,000 people took significant risks to cross the border for freedom.

Initially, people used buildings like border houses to escape across roofs and through windows into the West. The border authorities soon caught wind of this, forcing residents to move and sealing up the buildings along the borders.

They then assembled a permanent barrier through Berlin. The 27-mile-long Berlin wall was two fortress-like walls with an area described as the "death strip" between them. This area was bristled with landmines, barbed wire, attack dogs, and East German patrols; however, it frightened most East Berliners into staying where they were.

Chapter Seven

A Symbol of the Iron Curtain

When on 13 August 1961, the Communist administration of the German Democratic Republic began building their barbed wire "Antifaschistischer Schutzwall" between the two halves of Berlin, the official basis for the Wall was to stop Western "fascists" from permeating East Germany and weakening the socialist state. Nonetheless, its primary success was in curbing the vast number of defections from East to West. The Berlin Wall "remains one of the most important and lasting reminders of the Cold War."

West Berlin. "A bone in the Soviet throat."

The existence of capitalist West Berlin in the heart of East Germany was a constant source of tension in Soviet circles. It was a reminder that the Allied powers, who represented a completely different ideology to the

Soviet one, were flaunting their Western ideas and attracting honest, hard-working East Berliners to bright lights and freedom, which they should have rejected on their own.

On 22 October 1961, a dispute between an East German guard and an American bureaucrat who was going to the opera in East Berlin nearly caused a war. American and Russian tanks had a face-off at Checkpoint Charlie for most of the day before both backed down.

The 1948 Soviet siege of West Berlin was intended to starve the Allies. Instead of departing, however, the US and allies stocked their areas of the city by plane. This undertaking, the Berlin Airlift, lasted for longer than a year and provided more than 2.3 million tons of fuel, food, and other provisions to the City. In 1949 the Soviet Union ceased the blockade.

After a calm decade, friction arose again in 1958. For three years, the Soviet Union, made bold by the triumphant Sputnik satellite launch, which boosted their space race, and engaged by the flow of refugees to the West, made constant threats. Failed meetings occurred, and summits achieved nothing. Three million people went across to the West. In 1961, the Soviets had had enough, and without warning, they placed the initial barbed wire barrier.

Before the building of the wall, Berliners from either side of the city could travel around with largely restricted freedom. They were able to cross the East-West border post to go to work or to shop. They would go to the movies or the theater. Regular trains and subways transported passengers backward and forwards between the two halves. After the building of the wall, however, it became almost impossible to come from East into West Berlin except through one of the three famous checkpoints. These were at Helmstedt ("Checkpoint Alpha"), at Dreilinden ("Checkpoint Bravo"), and, the most famous or notorious of all, in the very heart of Berlin at Friedrichstrasse ("Checkpoint Charlie"). Eventually, the German Democratic Republic built 12 checkpoints along the wall. East German sentries screened all people at the checkpoints before they were authorized to enter or depart. It was only under special conditions that visitors from East or West Berlin were allowed to cross the boundary.

It's straightforward to see, from the Soviet perspective, how the division of East and West Berlin was never going to be a success without the Wall to enforce it, and that came at a significant cost.

Chapter Eight

The Mauerfall

The fall of the Berlin Wall, or the Mayerfall, occurred on 9 November 1989.

The Peaceful Revolution

In 1989, the communist government of East Germany was overpowered by the strong sentiments of democratization that swept across communist Eastern Europe. As a result, on 9 November 1989, East Germany proclaimed a relaxation of travel constraints to the West, and at once, thousands of people insisted on gaining passage through the Berlin Wall. Confronted with heightened demonstrations, the border guards from East German opened the border. Ecstatic Berliners clambered up on top of the Wall, painted it with graffiti, and removed pieces as souvenirs. The following day, soldiers from East Germany began disassembling the wall.

In 1990, on a day of great joy, East and West Germany were reunited after so many years at Bernauer Strasse.

The Peaceful Revolution, which is called the Friedliche Revolution in German, was part of a wide range of revolutions in 1989, where the Soviet Union split apart, but countries incorporated within it no longer wished to belong to the community and socialist regime. It brought about the opening of borders between East and West Germany and the "transition to democracy which enabled the reunification of Germany in 1990." This was brought about through peaceful demonstrations. The German people refer to this peaceful change as "Die Wenda," which means the turning point.

The changes that occurred during the Peaceful Revolution were climatic events in the modern world that featured the fall of the Iron Curtain and were one of the unstoppable series of incidents that began the fall of communism in Central and Eastern Europe. This was started by the Polish Solidarity Movement and was followed by the fall of the East/West German border. The Malta Summit from 2 and 3 December 1989 brought the Cold War to an end.

The End of the Wall.

In 1989, the communist government of East Germany was overpowered by the strong sentiments of democratization that swept across communist Eastern Europe. As a result, on 9 November 1989, East Germany proclaimed a relaxation of travel constraints to the West, and at once, thousands of people insisted on gaining passage through the Berlin Wall. Confronted with heightened demonstrations, the border guards from East German opened the border. Ecstatic Berliners clambered up on top of the Wall, painted it with graffiti, and removed pieces as souvenirs. The following day, soldiers from East Germany began disassembling the wall. In 1990, on a day of great joy, East and West Germany were reunited after so many years.

The Wall actually fell because of a bureaucratic error. In response to the revolutionary pressure, the East German Government planned to make getting visas easier to facilitate people going across the border. In reality, because of mixed messages, thousands of people streamed through the border post, cheering and sobbing, in scenes that were shown around the world. Many people climbed onto the wall at the Brandenburg gate and chipped away pieces of it with pickaxes and hammers.

Chapter Nine

Was the End of the Wall, a success for the German People

After the fall of the Berlin Wall, the 18 million people from East Germany were, after four years, able to travel to the West again, use their right to freedom of speech without anxiety about secret police and choose a democratically elected government.

However, according to a current opinion poll, only 38% of people from Eastern Germany considered the reunification of Germany to be successful.

The origins of this feeling of estrangement can be traced to what occurred in the eastern states of Germany after the Wall fell.

Claudia Haley

Claudia, a tour guide at the Schoeneweeide Industrial Museum in East Berlin, had the following to say. "It was a big economic and cultural shock. Many people here in the east felt lost," She explained that under the GDR, everyone had had a job in which they stayed. There was never a struggle for employment. "And that's what the older easterners who come here today tell us: 'I miss the feeling of being in a group at work.' They lost that feeling after the Wall came tumbling down," Haley explains to the tourists who visit the museum.

Hundreds of state-owned businesses were sold to private companies after the reunification and numerous of those collapsed because they could not compete in a capitalist market economy with a strong currency. Workers whose jobs were lost felt as if they were being victimized by the new, cruel and demanding, West German owners.

Mario Tiesies

Mario runs a charity supporting children from poor and disadvantaged families, and he explains the feeling of the old Easterners as "a widespread feeling of distrust." He explains that parents who bring their children lost out during the reunification. "Their parents never worked again. And they've never had a steady job," Tiesies explained. He went on to explain that although everybody gained freedom when the wall collapsed, they had lost much economic security. "There is a widespread feeling of distrust, a feeling that plenty of Westerners came here just to make easy money," he said.

There is a widespread belief in the Eastern states that, over the last 30 years, Easterners have been treated as "second-class citizens," explained economist Jörg Roesler. He feels that Western companies have plundered their Eastern colleagues. He believes the West "threw the East to the wolves." He felt that the Western tax money was wasted, and if Eastern European companies had been protected from competition from Western companies for just five years, then the scenario would have been very different. "A whole generation would not have been thrown out of work and made to feel worthless."

The problem is cultural and social as well as economical. Because the best, most mobile, motivated people escaped to the West early and did not go through 40 years of political oppression and sheltered employment, the Westerners were equipped to handle a market economy far more effectively than their Eastern counterparts.

It's a problem that only time and the rise of a united younger generation can heal.

Chapter Ten

The Berlin Wall Today

If you were to visit Berlin today, you would almost certainly want to see the remains of the Berlin Wall.

The Guided Tour

A tourist has to have quite a good imagination to visualize the Berlin Wall, for only a few remnants still exist. It's interesting to know where to find portions of the real wall and which edifices are only replicas of the famous wall. In several locations, metal plates set into the ground are reminders of where the Wall was situated.

An excellent beginning point for touring the Wall is the Berlin Wall Memorial which is at 111 Bernauer Straße., where the effects of the wall's construction have been extremely harsh. The Wall segregated neighbors and even families who were living very few blocks apart from one another. In the early days, some East Berliners escaped to the West by jumping out through windows in buildings adjoining the wall. The West Berlin fire department rescued them in a life net. After that, the windows in the buildings were bricked up, and the buildings were demolished.

Today, the tourist can visit the Documentation Centre (Wall Memorial), which has a fascinating photo exhibition exhibiting how the Brandenburg Gate barbed wire closed in August 1961 and how Berliners rioted against the Wall. It also has some moving photos of how desperate family and friends stretched their hands out across the perimeter barriers to touch one another

The fact that the initial boundary defenses soon evolved into much more than a wall can be observed from the fascinating viewing platform, which overlooks the area outside the Wall Memorial. Here, the tourists can witness the light pole foundations that brightly lit the border at night. The tourist can also see the signal fence posts. These would trigger an alarm if touched.

The Wall Trail would then take the tourist past the Reichstag, where a number of white crosses commemorate those who died trying to cross the wall. These can be seen on the corner of Scheidemannstraße. Even today, flowers and candles underlie the crosses to remind tourists of the real tragedies which played out.

There is also a 200-meter-long piece of the original wall still standing on Niederkirchnerstraße. It's protected as a historical monument.

In Friedrichshain, the section of the original wall is elaborately painted with graffiti. The area, which is 1.3 kilometers long, is called the East Side Gallery. This is because the Wall on the East side was painted by 118 artists representing 21 countries in 1990.

The paintings reveal the happiness and atmosphere of excitement of the time when the Wall fell, and the Cold War officially ended. The motifs show barbed wire, rising suns, doves as peace symbols, and broken chains. The world-famous picture of the Trabi, a small German car with the number plate "Nov. 9-89," breaks through the wall. Tourists love to be photographed in front of the graffiti wall.

Checkpoint Charlie

A famous destination for tourists doing the Wall trail is Checkpoint Charlie, situated in Kreuzberg. This was the former border post from West to East Berlin. In front of the "Mauermuseum," which was founded in 1962, j there is a fragment of the original wall and an original border post. The white building of the checkpoint on the western border is only a replica, but tourists can pay young men costumed in US or Russian uniforms to be photographed for money.

If you ever visit Berlin, you should take the Wall Tour and immerse yourself in a fascinating period of history.

Chapter Eleven

Conclusion

The Berlin Wall symbolized the ideological and government styles of the Eastern bloc, particularly the USSR and the Western powers of England, France, and the USA.

Soon after WWII, tensions between the previous allies indicated their ideologies were utterly incompatible. And it was evident from the very beginning that the communist and socialist systems in the East were not favorably compared by their citizens to the capitalist West, which offered far more choices and freedom.

While the border was easy to cross, as many as a thousand East Berliners defected a day, leaving the East German government and the USSR extremely frustrated. The wall was seen by many as a failure of the Soviet Union to offer people the lifestyle that they desired.

The Soviet Union saw the West as decadent and immoral and tried to prevent people from leaving to protect their citizens from the Westerners, whom they described as fascists.

It is a point of interest to note that countries with repressive and dictatorial regimes, like North Korea, China, and Russia, often use the excuse that they are protecting their citizens from harmful ideologies by reducing their contact with Western influences. This almost always brings citizens to the point of frustration, which eventually leads to rebellion against the repressive system. The objection to letting people form their own opinions and allowing them to choose their own religion, political affiliations, and freedom of expression is typical of an oppressive regime, and one is aware that the population will eventually object as they did during the Peaceful Revolution to force change by refusing to accept the current system anymore.

The Berlin Wall falling was also part of a broader peaceful revolution. The Czechs conducted the famous Velvet Revolution, which compelled the communist administration to declare the end to one-party rule. The Baltic states had the Baltic Chain, in which two million people held hands, forming a 675.5-kilometer human chain to demand liberation from the USSR.

Ultimately people showed that they were not prepared to accept an oppressive system in which they were both nannied and persecuted. The fall of that most impressive symbol, the Berlin Wall, gave hope to many that oppression could be defeated and the actual voice of the citizens could be heard.

Chapter Twelve

"Discuss with Friends and Family"

Discussion Question

The Berlin Wall has been called the concrete version of the Iron Curtain. Explain the difference between the two. Do you agree with that opinion?

Discussion Question

The division of Germany after WWII was very punitive. Do you think it was effective? What problems arise because of the Potsdam and Yalta agreements?

Discussion Question

Why did the East German authorities decide to build the wall? Was it an overreaction? Yes or no?

Discussion Question

What do you know about the involvement of American presidents in the matter of the Wall? List a few examples. Do you think they had an influence?

Discussion Question

Did the East Germans feel happy after reunification? What's your opinion? Was it good for the East Germans or not?

Discussion Question

A piece of the wall ended up in the Vatican gardens. What other odd place did a portion of the wall end up in? What's your opinion about that? Disrespectful or entertaining?

Discussion Question

Fewer than 200 people were killed crossing the wall. Nonetheless, the wall was seen as a major symbol of oppression. Why do you think this is the case?

Discussion Question

What crazy ways did people try to cross the wall? List some examples.

Would you have attempted escape or chosen the route of least

resistance?

Chapter Thirteen

"Test Your Knowledge"

Quiz Question

1. **True/False:** According to the East German authorities, the wall's name was the "Anti-Fascist Protective Wall" It was described as protecting the citizens from Western Fascism..

2. **True/False:** The area between the two walls was filled with dogs and tripwires. There was a moat filled with crocodiles. People also could stumble down holes into dungeons.

3. **True/False:** The most famous or notorious checkpoint of all was Checkpoint Charlie. It was in the very heart of Berlin at Friedrichstrasse.

4. **True/False:** On 26 June 1963, Kennedy apparently addressed a crowd at the Wall with the words "Ich bin ein Berliner." This translated as "I am a jelly donut."

5. **True/ False:** The Wall actually fell because of a bureaucratic error. The administrator was meant to tell the citizens that there would be an easing of border control. Instead, he said the border would open immediately.

6. **True/False:** The 1948 Soviet siege of West Berlin was intended to force the allies to attack the Russians. They wanted them to start a war so the Russians could fight without being the aggressor.

7. **True/False:** The Peaceful Revolution forced the end of the Iron Curtain. The Soviet Union was forced to give in to public pressure. This was from many nations making up the Soviet Union.

8. **True/ False:** The La Belle disco tragedy was caused by Soviet snipers. It nearly caused a war. It was seen as a direct attack on America.

Quiz Answer

1. True

2. False. There were dogs, mines, and armed guards, but no crocodiles or dungeons.

3. True

4. False. He said words that could colloquially be translated as a jelly donut. No one, however, seriously believed that was his intention.

5. True.

6. False. The Russians were trying to force the Allies to retreat. They hoped to starve them out. The Allies delivered food and supplies by plane.

7. True

8. False. It was a Libyan terrorist attack. The East German secret police might have been involved. The Libyans paid compensation, though.

Final Words From the Author...

Dear Reader,

It was my utmost privilege performing a deep dive to bringing this book for you today.

Before saying goodbye, I'd like to take opportunity to offer you one final gift. If you've enjoyed this book, may I ask for a small review?

If you do, I'll send you for FREE a most cherished and valuable gift as a way of showing my utmost appreciation:

Bestsellers Top 7 Treasure Box

These are my personal bestsellers sold at bookstores valued at ~$30USD, my gift to you absolutely FREE.

To claim your gift:

1. Leave a review where the book was purchased
2. Send a screenshot to irvinepress@mail.com
3. Receive your gift of **Bestsellers Top 7 Treasure Box**

Sincerely,

History Encounters

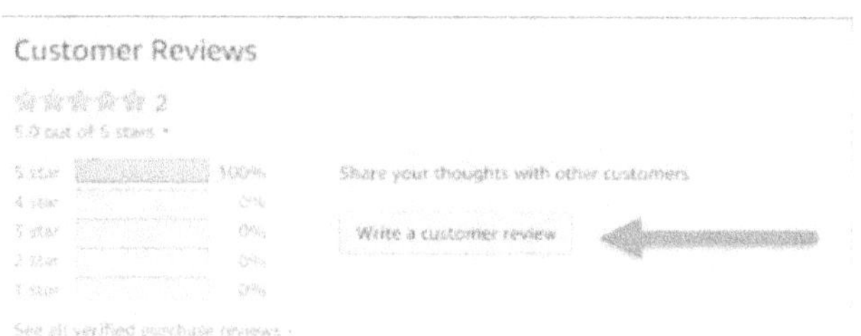

THANK YOU